I Can Take A Bath

Written by Chemise Taylor

Illustrated by Alexis B. Taylor

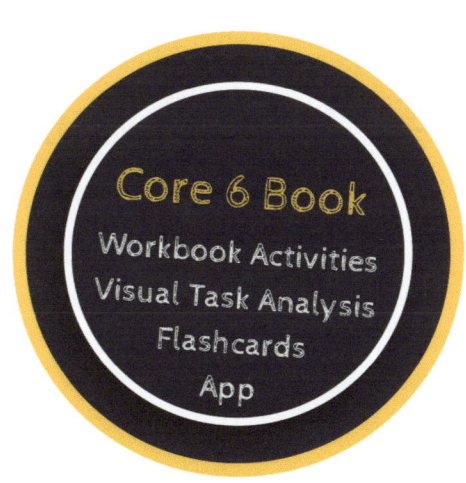

Copyright © 2019 by My Skills Books

Published by My Skills Books

All rights reserved. No part of this publication may be reproduced, distributed, or transmitted in any form or by any means, including photocopying, recording, or other electronic or mechanical methods, without the prior written permission of the publisher, except in the case of brief quotations embodied in critical reviews and certain other noncommercial uses permitted by copyright law.

First Printing, 2019.

ISBN: 978-1-951573-10-2

www.myskillsbooks.com

It's time to take a bath.

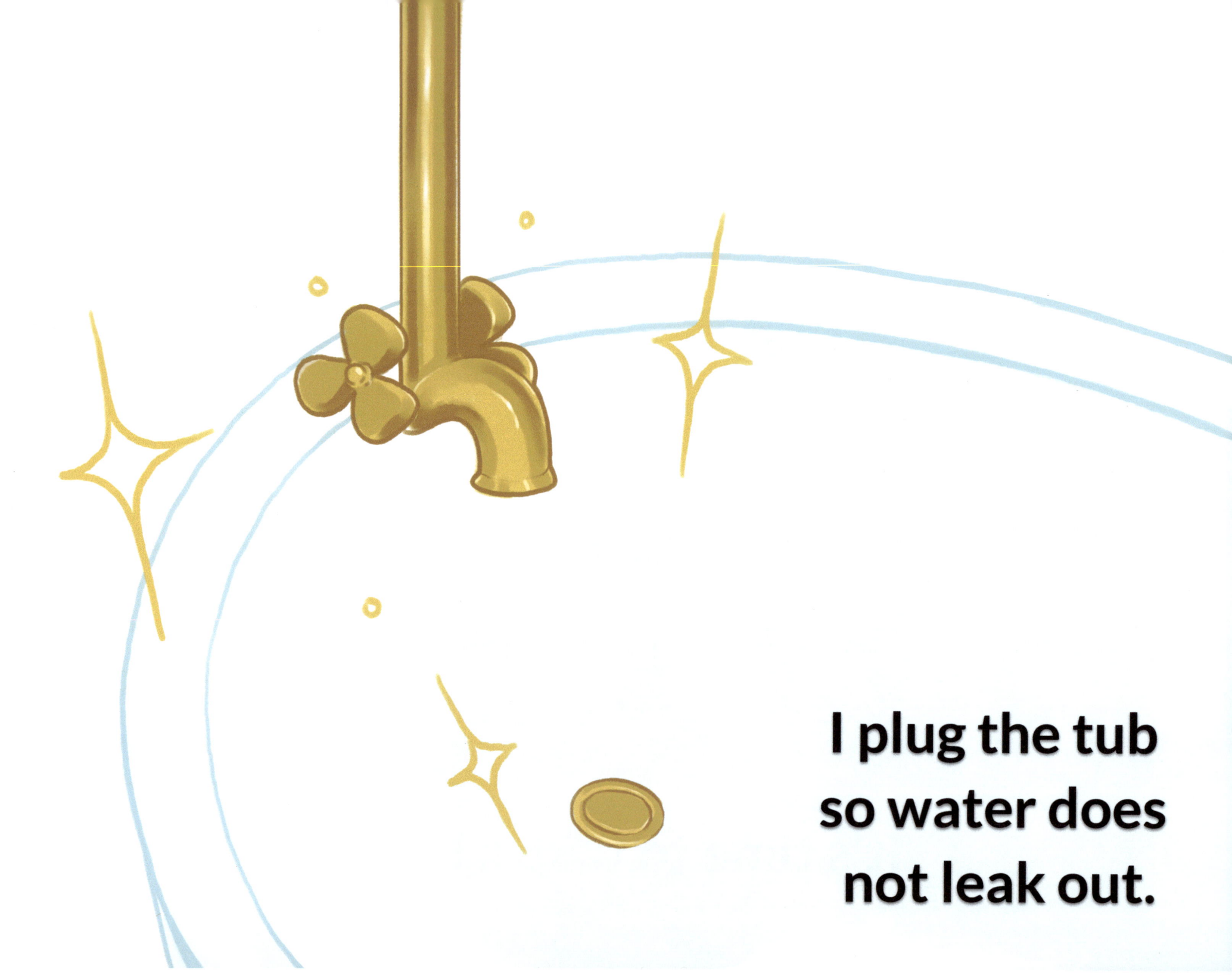

I plug the tub so water does not leak out.

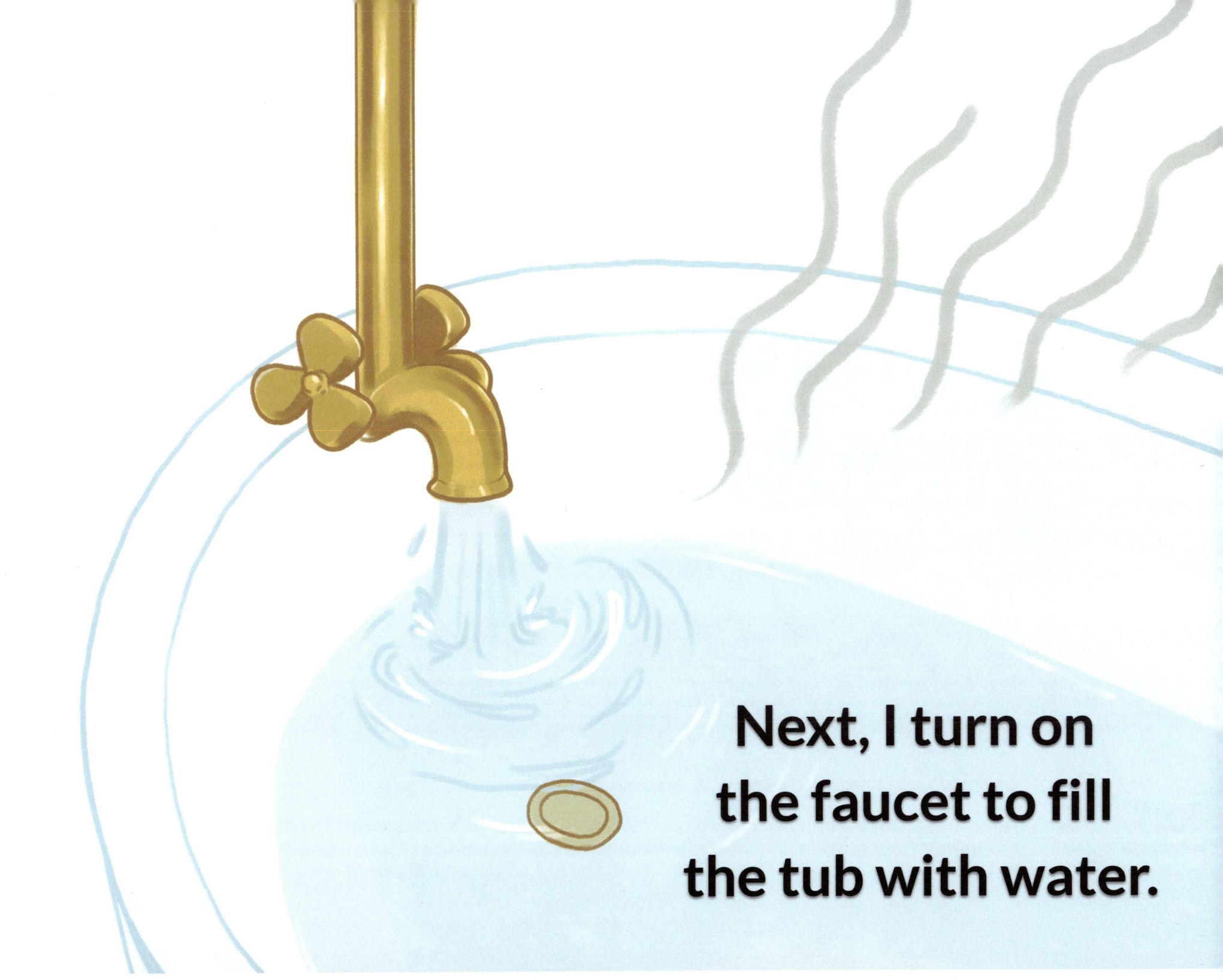

Next, I turn on the faucet to fill the tub with water.

I test the water to make sure it is not **too hot** or **too cold**.

Then, I squeeze my favorite bubble bath soap into the water.

I get into the bubble-filled tub.

Taking a bath is so much fun!

I wash my body with soap and water.

Now that I am all clean, I get out the tub and dry off with a towel.

After drying off, I put lotion on my skin.

I unplug the tub and watch the water disappear.

Then, I get dressed!

All done!

Book Details

Story Word Count: 121

Key Words: Bath, Tub, Soap, Clean, Wash, Squeeze, Fill, Plug

Comprehension Check
- What was the story about?
- What did he put in the tub?
- What did he do after he got out of the tub?

Reading Award

This certificate goes to:

_____

for reading "I Can Take A Bath"

Good Job!

More books, apps and resources at myskillsbooks.com

www.ingramcontent.com/pod-product-compliance
Lightning Source LLC
Chambersburg PA
CBHW042110090526

44592CB00004B/78